STOCK OPTIONS - THE APPLICATION OF DECISION THEORY TO BASIC AND ADVANCED STRATEGIES

James B. Cloonan Ph.D.

QUANTITATIVE DECISION SYSTEMS, INC.
CHICAGO, ILLINOIS

TO EDIE

TABLE OF CONTENTS

PREFACE

The interest in stock options which had been gradually increasing over the last two decades was catapulted upward by the introduction of stock options on the Chicago Board of Trade. The Chicago Board Options Exchange (CBOE) has contributed to the respectability of options, but, more importantly, provides a continual and standardized secondary market. As the list of options traded continues to grow and the daily volume sets new highs it is becoming apparent that the stock option has become a major investment vehicle.

No mature investor should be without an understanding of the stock option and the many roles it can play in investment planning. While it is true that the stock option provides high leverage for the speculator, it can also be among the most conservative of investments. This book considers both the speculative and conservative uses of stock options, but emphasis is given to the latter since the conservative strategies offer more opportunity for scientific analysis.

This book looks for a compromise between the theoretical and mathematical approach to options found in academic journals and the rather descriptive and non-specific contents of most books on stock options. A book on stock options cannot be meaningful without discussion of specific strategies and their mathematical rationale, but it is the author's feeling that most mathematical concepts required can be described in non-technical fashion and that the few imperative mathematical concepts can be clearly explained. This book will require some effort on the part of the reader, but it will give him a better understanding of option strategies and opportunities than possessed by many professional analysts.

The first chapter investigates some of the concepts of decision theory that are essential for the examination of investment strategies. This is followed in the second chapter by a general description of the stock option and the categorization of different option uses. Chapters 3, 4, and 5 consider different levels of conservative option strategies, and Chapters 6 and 7 examine speculative option opportunities. Chapter 8 discusses margin requirements and tax consequences.

Throughout the book various studies of options are referenced and the author owes a debt of gratitude to the many scholars whose work has led to the current state of option investment research.

Finally, every reader should recognize that the various estimates of profit potential discussed in this book are estimates of average expectations. Options are related to common stocks and there is no way to be certain of potential profits, particularly in the short run. The description of risk in the first chapter should be carefully studied. For those willing to accept risk for the chance of high returns the contents of this book should help to put the odds on your side.

James B. Cloonan   July 1, 1973
Chicago, Illinois

STOCK OPTIONS

THE APPLICATION OF DECISION THEORY

TO BASIC AND ADVANCED STRATEGIES

CHAPTER ONE

DECISION THEORY AND RISK

"There is no certainty regarding the future." That one statement sums up the nature of a probabilistic world — a world where we can never be certain of the results of our decisions. Because the future is uncertain, those who would make rational decisions must deal with probability and risk. This is true whether the area of interest is a Las Vegas Casino, a loan company, the weather, medical diagnosis, business decisions, or the stock market. As a background for an examination of stock options it is necessary to consider the nature of probability and risk.

While the discussion in this book will generally be at a non-technical level, a few concepts should be explained and some notation that will be used throughout the book defined.

MODEL

A model is an artificial way of representing something in real life. Model airplanes, pictures, and words themselves are examples of models, but of more importance is the concept of representing real life by a mathematical model such as:

$$A = B \times C$$

where — A is the area of a rectangle in square units
B is the length of a side in units
C is the length of the side adjacent to B in units

This is a mathematical model of the real world situation where it is true that the area of a rectangular surface is found by multiplying the lengths of two adjacent sides.

A more general form of a mathematical model, which will be used extensively in this book, is the functional notation f( ). The example of the area of a rectangle is a specific representation of how A (area) is determined from B and C (the two adjacent sides). A more general terminology is:

$$A = f (B,C)$$

which means that A (area) can be determined from B and C, but it does not state specifically how the determination is made. This notation X = f ( ) will be used and it indicates that X (whatever it may be) is determined by whatever is in the brackets after "f".

PROBABILITY MODELS

In describing the results of a particular course of action it could be stated that: *"If* A occurs *then* Z will occur." This would be a model of *certainty.* An example might be: *"If* I fully depress the accelerator of my car *then* the car will accelerate at a specific speed (given other circumstances)."

If what will happen is not known or there are a number of possible results then the model is *uncertain.* For example:

If I am sick and take these unlabeled pills
then I will get better
　or I will get worse
　or I will stay the same.

If there are a number of possible results and the likelihood of each result is known then the model is *probabilistic* For example:

If I toss this fair coin
then It will come up heads p (Heads)= .5
　or It will come up tails p (Tails)= .5

The requirements for a probabilistic model that is complete are that:
　　1. All possible results are listed.
　　2. The probability of each result is known or can be estimated. The probabilities are stated as decimal fractions between 0 and 1.0 where 0 means the result is impossible and 1.0 means it is certain. A 50-50 chance is written p = .5
　　3. The sum of the probabilities of all events must be 1.0.
The probability distribution of results of a particular course of action (pD) is the listing of all possible results that can occur and their expected frequencies, expressed in the fraction of time they will occur. Thus the probability distribution of a fair coin toss is:

$$\text{p D (coin toss)} = \begin{array}{l} .5 - \text{Heads} \\ .5 - \text{Tails} \end{array}$$

Stock Options

All decisions regarding investments are basically models under uncertainty. If the possible outcomes and the probability of each outcome are known then they are probabilistic models. Probabilistic models are the best that can be hoped for in investment decisions. *There is no certainty*. Investment decisions or business decisions are not unlike gambling, but a trip to Las Vegas should convince anyone that there is profit to be made from gambling if the odds are on your side (as they are for the casino). Decision making under conditions of probability is based on an effort to determine what the odds (probabilities) are, and when they favor you.

EXPECTED VALUE (EV)

With the description of a probabilistic model out of the way, consideration can be given to decision making under probabilistic conditions. Given knowledge of outcomes and a basis for decision (generally profit) it is relatively easy to make decisions under certainty. For example, given two stocks to choose from and certain outcomes,

	Outcomes
Buy Stock A	$1000 profit
or Buy Stock B	$2000 profit

it is easy to make a choice if profit is the criteria. Expanding the notion of probabilistic outcomes to a similar problem such as,

4

	Outcomes	Probability
	+$2000	.3
Buy Stock A	+$1000	.4
	-$1000	.3
	+$3000	.2
or Buy Stock B	+$ 100	.5
	-$2000	.3

it is somewhat more difficult to see which decision is best. Actually the method of choosing between Stock A and Stock B depends on two factors — the average return and the decision makers attitude toward risk. The first, average return or expected profit will be considered here and a discussion of risk will follow in the next section.

The expected value of the two alternatives is the average expected profit if the decision was made a great number of times. It is calculated by multiplying each outcome by its probability of occurring and summing the results. In the case of Stock A vs. Stock B the results are as follows:

Buy Stock A

Outcomes(O)	Probability(P)	P x O
+$2000	.3	$600
+$1000	.4	$400
-$1000	.3	-$300
Total	1.0	$700 = Expected Profit (EP)

Stock Options

<u>Buy Stock B</u>

<u>Outcomes(O)</u>	<u>Probability(P)</u>	<u>P x O</u>
+$3000	.2	$600
+$ 100	.5	$ 50
-$2000	.3	-$600
Total	1.0	$ 50 = Expected Profit (EP)

One more example is given concerning the choice between three stock purchases. The outcomes and their probabilities are listed. The reader should try to calculate the EP for each choice before looking at the solution.

	<u>$ Outcomes</u>	<u>P</u>	<u>P x O</u>
Stock A	+3000	.25	
	+2000	.25	
	+1000	.25	
	-2000	.25	
	Total	1.00	= EP
Stock B	+2000	.25	
	+ 100	.50	
	-2000	.25	
	Total	1.00	= EP
Stock C	+5000	.4	
	+ 250	.2	
	-5000	.4	
	Total	1.0	= EP

As is required the probabilities of all outcomes for each stock total 1.0, indicating that all possibilities are covered. Obviously, more than 3 or 4 outcomes are possible but the number has been kept down for simplicity. However it is common to select a limited number of outcomes, each of which represents the average of a group. For example, in the case of Stock B, + 2000 might be the average result for the stock moving up 10% or more, while + 100 might be the average of the stock being between + 10% and -8%.

The calculation of EV for the three stocks A, B, and C follows:

Stock A EV = .25 x 3000 + .25 x 2000
               + .25 x 1000 + .25 x -2000
           = 750 + 500 + 250 -500
           = \$1000

Stock B EV = .25 x 2000 + .5 x 100
               + .25 x -2000
           = 500 + 50 -500
           = \$50

Stock C EV = .4 x 5000 + .2 x 250 + .4 x -5000
           = 2000 + 50 − 2000
           = \$50

On this basis Stock A has the highest EV and, subject to the discussion of risk that follows, would be the best choice.

RISK

Simply stated, risk is the probability of incurring a loss. Few investment decisions are free from at least one outcome that represents a loss and thus there is usually some risk in every decision. To examine the nature of risk the probability distribution of four investment opportunities will be examined. The first is a situation of certainty and the other three are probabilistic. Outcomes are expressed in gain or loss on investment. It should be noted that few people would accept the chance of a loss (risk) without reason and greater risk usually is accompanied by the chance of greater gain.

	Outcomes	P	P x O
Keep money in drawer	0	1.0	0
	Total	1.0	0
Stock A	+10,000	.3	3000
	0	.4	0
	-10,000	.3	-3000
	Total	1.0	0 = EV
Stock B	+ 5,000	.3	1500
	0	.4	0
	- 5,000	.3	-1500
	Total	1.0	0 = EV
Stock C	10,000	.15	1500
	0	.7	0
	-10,000	.15	-1500
	Total	1.0	0 = EV

8

Examining these alternatives it can be seen that keeping the money in a drawer involves no probability and no risk, thus it is the safest of the alternatives. By almost any standard Stock A involves more risk than Stock B because A has the same probability of a greater loss. In evaluating Stock C it can be seen that it has the same dollar risk as A, (the decider can loose $10,000), but his probability of loss is lower. It seems reasonable to say that Stock C involves less risk than Stock A. In general it is safe to say that if the potential losses are equal, the choice with the lowest probability of that loss involves less risk. It can also be said that if the probabilities of loss in choices are equal, the choice with the lowest dollar loss is less risky. It is not possible to compare the risk of Stock B with Stock C. The question becomes — Is a 15% chance of losing 10,000 more or less risky than a 30% chance of loosing 5,000? The answer depends on the attitude of individuals towards risk-taking.

The solution to the last posed problem can be solved by analysis of the decision makers utility for money. This subject will not be covered because it is not essential. Those interested in this subject may read reference (9). Generally speaking people are risk preferers, risk neutral, or risk avoiders. If individuals are asked what they would pay for a .5 chance of winning $100, the risk neutral person would pay $50 (the EV), the risk avoider would only be willing to pay less than $50, and the risk preferer will pay more than $50 as attested by the people who play roulette against the house.

The analysis of risk will not be carried further. It is important to note, however, that, 1) Decision choices may be different because of the difference in risk even though expected profit (EP) is the same, 2) The degree of risk is frequently based on personal attitudes. There is no general way of determining whether a 20% chance of loosing $5000 is more risky than a 10% chance of loosing $10,000, and 3) Individuals do not necessarily exhibit the same attitudes towards risk at different times or under different conditions. For example, the same person who buys insurance and thus pays a premium to avoid risk may later visit a casino where he pays a premium to accept risk. Obviously, few people prefer risk for its own sake and risk normally implies a corresponding opportunity for greater gain.

DIVERSIFICATION AND RISK REDUCTION

While different individuals may react to risk differently, diversification or repetition can reduce risk. The effect of diversification or repetition can be seen by an example of coin tossing. If two games of coin tossing are examined:

Game 1	Win	$5	P = .5	$2.50 ($5 x .5)
	Lose	-$5	P = .5	-2.50 (-5 x .5)
				0 = EP
Game 2	Win	$10	P = .5	$5.00 ($10 x .5)
	Lose	-10	P = .5	-5.00 (-10 x .5)
				0 = EP

10

It can be seen that the EP of each is equal, but based on the previous discussion Game 2 involves more risk. However if Game 2 is played 10 or 100 times the probability distributions of the possible outcomes may appear less risky than the outcomes of Game 1. Once again the evaluation of risk is subjective, but given a particular individual's attitudes about risk it is frequently possible that a diverse portfolio of speculative investments will exhibit less risk than a single "blue chip."

ECONOMIC VS ACCOUNTING LOSS

The previous discussion has treated loss and thus risk of loss in terms of actual accounting (or tax) results. Such an approach can often be misleading because it fails to take into account the alternate use of investment funds. The individual who makes a stock investment of $5000 and two years later realizes $5300 will generally say he has made a profit on the stock market. The government requires that he report the $300 gain and if he keeps books he has indeed made an accounting gain. In decision theory however, it is better to look at the economic gain or loss, which is, "How do the results compare to the next best alternative?" If the individual above took money out of a savings account yielding 6% then the following comparison should be made.

Stock investment: 5000 becomes 5300, profit $300

No stock investment: 5000 becomes 5600,

profit $600 (ignoring compounding)
Economic (opportunity) loss on stock $300

Failure to consider opportunity loss can confuse evaluation of decision processes. While it is not always easy to precisely determine the alternative use, an investor when evaluating his results should, before saying "bad" or "good", ask — "compared to what."

NOT SELLING IS BUYING

The attitude that there is no loss (or gain) until it is realized is akin to thinking that people get a year older on their birthdays but don't age during the year. Except for tax purposes a gain or a loss is there whether it is realized (in a tax sense) or not. If a stock bought at 50 is now 30 it should not be held unless you would buy it at 30 in preference to all other investments. There is a small exception to this rule. That exception is — if your expectation for another investment is only enough better than the stock you hold to pay the commission then you should hold. The stock you hold may indeed go up again to 50, but if the $30 in another investment would have gone up more, there is an opportunity loss from holding. Decisions in this area should, of course, be based on profits or losses after tax considerations.

The preceding definitions and discussion should prepare the reader for an analytic investigation of options or any other investment opportunities. While complicated notation has not been used, the basic concepts necessary for understanding the analysis of options that follows have been covered. It is important that the reader understand these preliminary concepts before proceeding to the discussion of strategies in Chapter 3. Even if the reader never becomes involved in option trading the elements of decision theory covered should be of value in all areas of decision making.

CHAPTER TWO

AN INTRODUCTION TO THE STOCK OPTION

Examination of the nature of stock options is best begun by defining some basic terms.

Underlying Stock — The stock or other security on which an option is given.

Option — A contractual agreement allowing its purchaser to trade a set number of shares of the underlying stock (sometimes another security, i.e. warrant) at a specific price during a specific period of time regardless of the market price of the security.

Call — An option giving the option buyer the right to purchase the underlying security.

Put — An option giving the option buyer the right to sell the underlying security.

Straddle — A put and a call on the same security with identical terms.

Spread — In over-the-counter options the term "spread" has been used for a position of a put and a call with different striking prices. Since this option is rare, "spread" is now used for CBOE options to describe a position where an investor has bought and written options on the same stock with different expiration dates.

Other Options —

Other options are used or have been used but are not significant. Among these are the strip (2 puts and 1 call), the strap (2 calls and 1 put), and the "down and out" (a call with a cancellation provision if the underlying stock goes a set amount below the original striking price).

Writer —

The seller of the option. Writer or maker is used because in the over the counter option market the seller actually creates a new security — the option. In the listed (CBOE) market the seller is not really the issuer, but the term "writer" still prevails.

Holder —

The buyer of the option contract.

OTC Market — Options that are traded on an over the counter basis. OTC options may be on underlying stocks that are traded on listed exchanges (NYSE, ASE, etc.) or the underlying stock may also be OTC.

CBOE — The Chicago Board Options Exchange — a subsidiary of the Chicago Board of Trade. Options traded on this exchange are "listed".

Expiration Date — The date on which the option expires. OTC options are generally for 6 months 10 days or 95 days, but options are sometines issued for other lengths from 1 year to 35 days. CBOE options expire the last business day of January, April, July, and October. OTC options expire at 3:15 p.m. (New York time) on the expiration date. CBOE options expire at 2:15 p.m. (Chicago time) on the expiration date.

Striking Price — The price originally set in the option contract at which the buyer of a call can purchase the stock from the writer and at which the buyer of a put may sell his stock to the writer. On the OTC market the striking price is usually the market price of the underlying stock at the time the option is created. On the CBOE the striking prices are standardized.

Exercise Price — The price at which the buyer can effectively exercise his option is the striking price adjusted for certain occurrences during the life of the option. These occurrences are stock splits, stock dividends and reorganizations for the CBOE. In the case of OTC stocks, adjustment is also made for cash dividends. In the case of cash dividends the adjustment has the effect of giving the dividends to the option buyer if the option is exercised. In the case of splits, etc., the adjustment serves to treat the situation as if the option buyer had exercised his option when he bought it. Thus all changes in corporate structure that take place during the life of the option are for the account of the buyer — if he exercises the option.

Premium — The premium is often defined as the price the buyer pays the seller for the option. This is correct for CBOE options and commissions are subtracted for both parties in the transaction. In OTC options the brokers generally take a $37.50 — $62.50 spread in lieu of commissions so that the "premium paid" by the buyer will not be the same as the "premium received" by the seller.

Endorsement — In the case of OTC options a New York Stock Exchange member guarantees that the writer will meet his obligation. In the case of CBOE options the CBOE (through its Clearing Corporation) is obligated for fulfilling option contracts.

Secondary Market — In the case of OTC options there is sometimes the chance to buy or sell already existing options. A buyer can make "special offers" to sell or a writer can attempt to find a new writer for his position. The secondary market in OTC options is very spotty and generally writers must be prepared to honor their contract until the option expires.

Away from
Market — An option is said to be "away from the market" if the striking price is different than the market price at the time of purchase. Practically all CBOE options are away from the market. Generally only special offerings as described above are sold away from the market in the OTC market.

In the
Money — A call selling away from the market is said to be "in the money" if the current price of the underlying security is greater than the striking price. As would be expected such options sell for more than a similar option where the market price and striking price of the underlying security are the same. The opposite is true for a put.

Out of the
Money — A call selling away from the market is said to be "out of the money" if the current price of the underlying security is less than the

20

striking price. As would be expected such options sell for less than a similar option where the market price and striking price are the same. The opposite is true for a put.

OPERATIONS OF OPTION MARKETS

Basically OTC options are handled in much the same way as OTC stocks. Prospective Writers and Buyers call a broker that handles puts and calls (Many New York Stock Exchange Firms and a group of specialized Put and Call Dealers handle option transactions) indicating their interest in buying or writing options in various stocks. The different dealers in options compare their own lists for matches and then contact other dealers by phone or wire. In stocks where options are active the dealers are aware of going prices and only a little negotiation is necessary. In the case of less active options, bids or asks are solicited and the dealers negotiate a price acceptable to writer and buyer. The writer generally receives $37.50 to $62.50 less than the buyer pays, the balance going to the various dealers involved. The buy and sell spread depends on the number of dealers involved.

Options handled within a single firm generally involve a lesser spread. On actively traded options the dealer may be willing to buy an option before having found a customer buyer on the assumption a buyer will be easy to find. A dealer is more willing to do this on a straddle (a put and a call) since if the stock price moves a loss on the one side will be offset by a gain on the other. A dealer may also be willing to buy without a customer buyer if he feels that the "price is right," that is, he feels there is a reasonably good chance to find a buyer and he stands to make more than the normal spread. Dealers may also take a position, that is, write or buy options for their own account.

On the CBOE, options are handled very much like the securities on any exchange. Floor brokers representing houses that are members of CBOE match bids and offers on the exchange floor. Specialists in each option operate to maintain an orderly market and current trades are posted on the floor and reported on a tape transmitted to members' offices.

BACKGROUND

While the CBOE only came into existence in April 1973, OTC options have been traded in the United States and elsewhere for many years. The commodity option goes back thousands of years and some of the disastorous effects of abuses of commodity options, such as the tulip bulb fiasco that almost destroyed the economy of Holland in the 1600's, have served to give stock options a questionable reputation. There is no doubt that the improper uses of stock options from the late 1800's until 1934 also served to contribute to a questionable reputation and to efforts of the Congress to outlaw them. The Put and Call Brokers and Dealers Association, formed in 1934, has regulated the options market since that time. Since 1934 the put and call market has operated more or less with the same efficiency and self control as the OTC market in stocks.

As might be expected, during the recovery after the depression and through World War II, volume in Puts and Calls was small but during the 1950's volume grew until by 1960 option contracts were estimated as being equal to more that 1% of the volume on the New York Stock Exchange. While the CBOE is new, its volume has been increasing rapidly and is already equivalent to over 2% of the New York Stock Exchange volume with only a limited number of options listed.

The trend of OTC options and the initial success of the CBOE would seem to indicate that options are soon to be a very significant investment instrument and that even investors who do not plan on using options must be familiar with them.

THE USES OF OPTIONS

The uses of options are extremely varied, but they can be placed into three major categories: Speculative, Programmed and Hedging.

Speculative Uses — "Speculative" is not used in a derogatory sense. Any short term purchase of a stock must be considered speculative and since option durations are less than a year they are meant for short term trading. Speculative option trading has as its foundation a dependence on the movement of the underlying stock. The option has a different result but basically purchase of a call is similar to buying the underlying stock and purchase of a put is similar to the short sale of the stock. While the speculative use of options usually involves the purchase of options, it is occasionally possible to sell options to accomplish short term investment objectives. In any event the speculative use of options is based on the investor's faith that the underlying stock will move up or, in the case of a put, move down. Chapters 6 and 7 will be devoted to study of the speculative uses of options and to the making of appropriate option investment decisions.

Programmed Uses — The programmed use of options is almost completely restricted to option selling although exceptions to this will be found in the discussion of Strategies — Level III in Chapter 5. The programmed use of options requires a different outlook than the speculative use. The option writer with a programmed approach must think of himself as providing a service for a fee. His profit comes from the premiums he receives and he has little interest in the stocks on which he writes except that they not behave in such a way as to cause him loss. He frequently makes a profit at the same time as the buyer, so the buyer and seller are not in opposition. While the option writer hopes the stocks on which he writes will not behave in such a way that they cut into his profits, he does not count on the behavior of any one stock but writes on a diversified portfolio looking for average performance. To the same end he diversifies his writings through time, so any short period of bad (for him) stock market performance will not be disastrous. Basically the programmed use of options is a conservative investment strategy providing an attractive rate of return for limited risk. The rate and the level of risk are very dependent on the strategy used and the various writing strategies will be discussed in the next three chapters.

Hedging Uses — Options can also be used as a hedge for other investments. In this case the buyer of an option may well have taken a strong position in the underlying stock and wishes to hedge his commitment, or he may already have made a sizeable gain and wishes to lock it in. Since the hedging use of options will not be discussed at any length later in this book several examples will be covered here.

Example 1. Mr. X purchased 1000 shares of the stock of XYZ company in January, believing the stock ready to make a move. He paid $30 a share or $30,000 for the stock. By May the stock had moved to 50. At that price Mr. X still believes the stock can move up more but also fears a downside move which might eliminate his profits. Without the availability of options the best move might be to enter a stop loss order, say at 45, thus restricting his loss (relative to a price of 50) to $5000. An alternate plan is to buy 10 puts on XYZ at a striking price of 50, say for a premium of $500 each or $5000. Mr. X now can sell his shares to the writer at $50 anytime in the following 6-month period. As in the stop loss he limits his loss to $5000 but will still realize additional gain if the stock price moves up. There are, however, three interesting differences between the two protective strategies:

1. If the stock moves up without dropping to 45 the stop loss costs nothing while the $5000 expended on puts would be lost. Under these circumstances the stop loss would be better.

2. If the stock drops to 45 or less, both the stop loss and option purchase would appear to be equal but there is an interesting difference. If the stock drops to 45 and the stop loss is exercised prior to July the entire gain from 30 to 45 or $15,000 is short term. In the case of purchasing the puts, Mr. X would not exercise his right to sell until after six months had expired thereby realizing a long term gain. *

3. If the stock temporarily drops past 45 and then turns up to more than 50, the stop loss will have been exercised and Mr. X will not participate in the new gains. In the case of the puts Mr. X would hold them for their duration and if the stock went down and then up within the 6 month 10 day exercise period he will benefit from the additional gain.

Calls can be used to hedge short sales in the same way although the tax consequences will be different (See Chapter 8). Not much more will be said

---

* This tax advantage is no longer possible under current rules.

about the hedging uses of options, but such uses can be effective and should be remembered whenever there is a situation where one wishes to protect a stock position without liquidating it.

Specific approaches for the programmed and speculative use of options will be discussed in the following chapters.

CHAPTER THREE

CALL OPTIONS – LEVEL I STRATEGIES

The programmed approach to option writing emphasizes the writing of call options. Puts do not generally offer favorable opportunities for option writing. First, they are not currently available on the CBOE, but second and more important, the premiums for put options are not high enough to be attractive. Calls can be used when the writer is bearish or bullish. A hedged call presents the same risks as a naked put and a hedged put presents the same risks as a naked call, so as long as calls have higher premiums there is no incentive to write puts.

An exception to this is the writing of straddles (a combined put and call). There are several reasons for writing straddles.

1. They are easier to sell. A dealer may be willing to take them into inventory because holding a straddle involves virtually no risk.

2. Even though the premiums for puts are lower (½ to ¾) than for calls, the seller of a call can also sell an equivalent put for only slightly more margin (25%). Because of this leverage the return on investment can be as high for the put side of a straddle as for a call.

Since it has been shown that there is a demand for puts as hedging devices and it will be seen in later chapters that there are speculative uses for them, put buyers absorb many of the puts generated by the writing of straddles. Typically, however, there are more people wishing to write straddles than willing to buy puts. Balance is maintained by an interesting process called "conversion."

It is possible to change a put into a call. This process can be carried out by individuals but the commissions reduce profits and so conversion houses do most of the converting. Following is an example of how a put is converted to a call.

XYZ stock is selling at 50. Puts are bid at $400 and calls bid at $650. The converter buys a put, sells a call, and buys 100 shares of XYZ. The converter has no risk. If the stock goes up the call will be exercised but since the converter owns the stock he simply delivers it for no loss. If the stock goes down the converter will lose money on the stock but he will exercise his put for an offsetting gain. His profit is the difference between the $650 he received and the $400 he paid or $250. The converter has a risk free investment returning $250 less expenses for a six month investment of $5000. Obviously if the spread between a call and a put on the same stock gets wide there will be much conversion activity, as it narrows there will be less. Conversion keeps the relative prices of puts and calls within a narrow range and provides a put market for straddle writers.

Despite the margin advantages of writing straddles the strategies to be discussed do not recommend writing them. This posture is taken because the straddle strategies, particularly the advanced strategies, are not as efficient as call writing strategies. A second reason for avoiding straddle writing is the rather archaic regulations most brokerage houses have towards the put side. This situation results from the generally negative attitude towards short positions.

STRATEGY CONSIDERATIONS

Already a few terms relating to writing strategies have been used. The term "naked" means writing a put or call without any position in the underlying stock. The term "hedged" means holding a position in the underlying stock that can deliver against the option. In the case of a call option, being hedged means owning the shares that are optioned. This means that if the call is exercised no loss will take place. It should be noted, however, that if the stock moves down the writer will have a loss on the stock. In the case of a put, being hedged means having a short position in the stock. If the stock moves down and the put is exercised the short position will allow the writer to buy the shares and there will be no loss due to the exercise of the option. If the stock goes up, however, the writer will have a loss in his stock position. "Partially hedged" means that the writer has an offsetting position in the stock but for fewer shares than are optioned.

THE BASIC STRATEGIES

The basic or Level I call writing strategies are listed below.

S1 — Write call(s) without stock purchase (Naked)

S2 — Write call(s) and buy optioned stock (Hedged)

S3 — Write call(s) and buy part of optioned stock (Partially Hedged)

The investor using Level I strategies maintains his position until the option written is exercised or expires. The outcomes of different possible market conditions for each of the three strategies are summarized in Table 3.1.

Table 3.1 Results of Different Strategies Under Different Market Conditions

Strategy \ Market	Stock goes above striking price — option exercised.	Stock drops below striking price — option expires	Stock does not move significantly — option expires
S2 (Hedged)	+ Premium — Transaction costs Net gain.	+ Premium — Transaction costs — Loss on stock Gain if stock drops less than premium—loss if more.	+ Premium — Transaction costs Net gain.
S1 (Naked)	+ Premium — Transaction costs — Stock loss Gain if stock goes up less than premium—loss if more.	+ Premium — Transaction costs Net gain.	+ Premium — Transaction costs Net gain.
S3 (Partial Hedge)	Half S1 Half S2	Half S1 Half S2	Half S1 Half S2

Stock Options

To examine the nature of the strategies some examples follow.

Example A — S1 (Naked)

The investor writes options on 200 shares of XYZ Co. for $450 each. He does not buy XYZ stock selling at $30 which is the striking price. XYZ continues to go up throughout the 6 month 10 day option period and on the exercise date is selling at $36. The buyer of the option exercises and the investor must buy XYZ shares on the market at $36 and sell them to the buyer at $30. The writer's profit (loss) is:

Profit = Premium − Stock Loss − Transaction costs

-$486=900−1200−186 (commissions approximate)

Loss is $486

Example A — S2 (Hedged)

The situation is the same as the previous example except that the writer buys 200 shares of XYZ at 30 to hedge the options he has written. In this case the profit (loss) is:

Profit = Premium − Stock Loss − Transaction costs

$724 = 900−0−176 (commissions approximate)

Profit = $724

Example A — S3 (Half-hedge)

With the same situation suppose the writer only buys 100 shares to hedge the options for 200 shares. Then under the same circumstances:

34

Profit = Premium — Stock Loss — Transaction Costs

$119 = 900 − 600 − 181 (commissions approximate)

Profit = $119

Example B — S1 (Naked)

The investor writes options on 200 shares of XYZ Co. for $450 each. He does not buy XYZ stock selling at $30 which is the exercise price. XYZ slips gradually throughout the 6 month option period and on the exercise date is selling at 24. The option buyer does not exercise. The writer's profit (loss) is:

Profit = Premium — Stock Loss — Transaction Costs

$900 = 900 − 0 − 0

Profit = $900

Example B — S2 (Hedged)

The situation is the same as the previous example except the writer buys 200 shares of XYZ when he writes the options and sells them at the market price of 24 when the option expires:

Profit = Premium — Stock Loss — Transaction Costs

-$465 = 900 − 1200 − 165 (commissions)

Loss = $465

Example B — S3 (Half Hedge)

With the same situation suppose the writer only buys 100 shares to hedge the options for 200 shares and sells the 100 shares when the options expires:

Profit = Premium — Stock Loss — Transaction Costs

$208 = 900 − 600 − 92 (commissions)

Profit = $208

The results of the two examples can be summarized.

	Example A	Example B	Average
S1	-486	900	207
S2	714	-465	125
S3	119	208	164

Obviously S1 is best if the stock moves down, S2 is best if the stock moves up and S3 is the least risky if the investor is uncertain. One point should be brought out. Example A and Example B were exact opposites so on average it could be expected that S1, S2, and S3 would give equal average results. They do not because S1 will require fewer commissions, on average, than S2, and S3 falls in between. From this it is possible to discern that if, over a portfolio and over time, stock were equally likely to go up or down, S1 would be somewhat better than S2 because of the commission savings. S1 also has an additional advantage, assuming once again an equality of ups and downs, in that less money will be tied up in the underlying stocks. This can be seen as the return on investment (ROI) rather than the absolute gains are examined.

INVESTMENT AND RETURN

While the examples used are only illustrative and stock prices could move more or less then those shown, the examples are in a realistic range and will be used to show how the return on investment (ROI) can be calculated.

$$ROI = \frac{Profit\,(Loss)}{Investment} \times \frac{365}{Length\,of\,option\,(Days)}$$

The profit for each of the six possibilities has already been determined, now the amount of investment will be calculated. The figures will be based on the assumption of full payment rather than the use of margin. Later the effect of using margin will be discussed. Without the use of margin it can be assumed that if the stock is not purchased an equivalent amount will be held in reserve to purchase the stock if the option is exercised. Commissions will be ignored in terms of investment although they have been included in the calculation of profit. If margin is not used the investment is the same in all cases. Premiums are paid to the writer immediately and thus reduce the investment necessary to purchase the stock or maintain a reserve.

Investment = Stock Cost (or Reserve) — Premium
5100 = 6000 — 900

The ROI (annualized) can now be calculated for all six conditions. For S3 in Example A the profit was $119. The investment is $5100.

$$ROI = \frac{Profit\,(Loss)}{Investment} \times \frac{365}{Length\,of\,option\,(Days)}$$

$$= \frac{119}{5100} \times \frac{365}{192} = .044$$

Stock Options

Calculating the ROI for each of the six conditions provides the following ROI's which are included with the actual profit and loss in parenthesis.

	Example A	Example B	Average
S1	-.181 (-486)	.335 (900)	.077 (207)
S2	.266 (714)	-.173 (-465)	.047 (125)
S3	.044 (119)	.078 (208)	.061 (164)

The ROI in these examples ranges from +33% to -18% with an average of 6%. While the effect of margin will vary depending on current margin regulations, typically the use of margin will double the returns both positive and negative.

ACTUAL ROI

There have been a variety of estimates of the ROI from option writing using Level I strategies and they are contradictory. These studies (see references 2, 3, 6, 8, 9) indicate an average ROI of 0%, indicating there is no profitability in writing options under Level I strategies. While it is felt that Level I Stategies are inferior to the strategies discussed in later chapters; their efficiency is probably better than indicated by the reseach reports mentioned. The reason for this is that several of the studies include puts and calls which gives results lower than the results from writing calls alone. In addition some of the research assumes that calls would be written on stocks regardless of the offered premium,

38

while in actuality there is probably less writing when premiums are low, and thus actual writing is likely more successful than estimates of writing behavior. Research by the author, which will be covered in more detail in the next chapter, indicates that Level I strategies lose about 7% under adverse market conditions. Under ideal conditions the yields can be very high. While it is only an estimate, analysis of the various studies and estimates from option writers would tend to support the feeling that over a long period of time and with a diversity of stocks, Strategies Level I will yield from 6 — 12% depending on how much selectivity the writer exercises. This rate of return places call writing strategies Level I in the range of other investments and since they require considerably more effort, option writing can not be recommended if Level I Strategies are to be used.

LEVEL I VARIATIONS

Careful evaluation of the stocks on which options are written could undoubtedly increase the ROI of Level I strategies, but since better strategies are available such evaluation will be discussed with Strategies Level II and III.

Another technique that can be used with any strategies that involve hedging, is the use of a convertible security (convertible bonds, convertible preferred stocks, or warrants) to hedge the option.

Convertible Bonds have three advantages:

1. If in the right price range, which means

that the convertible bond is not too far above its bond value (value based on interest return), the convertible bond will offer better downside protection than the underlying stock itself.

2. The margin requirements are usually lower for convertible bonds and, based on a New York Stock Exchange ruling in 1972, convertible bonds are acceptable in lieu of stock as an option hedge.

3. Commissions per dollar are lower on bonds than on stocks. If the option is exercised, however, a stock commission will also have to be paid.

Convertible Preferred Stocks have the first advantage listed for bonds but not the other two.

Warrants do not have the advantages listed for convertible bonds or preferreds except that under certain conditions there is better downside protection. The major advantage of warrants is that they frequently offer increased leverage since they are usually less expensive than the equivalent stock. This leverage, however, works on both gains and losses. There are not a great number of opportunities to hedge with warrants since when they are available many potential option buyers will simply buy the warrant, thereby reducing the demand for calls.

The discussion of Level I strategies has been an introduction to option writing. As can be gathered from the analysis such approaches are not recommended for an option program.

CHAPTER FOUR
CALL OPTIONS — LEVEL II STRATEGIES

Level II Strategies begin the same as the Level I Strategies described in the previous chapter. The writer upon writing the options takes either a naked, hedged or partially hedged position. The writer, however, stands ready to adjust his hedged position based on the performance of the stock during the option period. A "D" will be added to the S1, S2, S3 for Level II Strategies indicating the initial position and the fact that defensive action will be taken. Definition of the strategies follows.

S1D

Initial — The writer starts from a naked position.

Defensive — The writer stays naked unless the stock moves up to a preset level, in which case he buys the stock. He continues to hold the stock unless it falls to another preset level.

Graphically the strategy is portrayed in Figure 4.1.

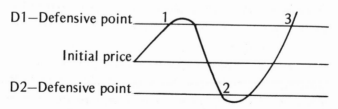

Figure 4.1. Strategy S1D — Limits

If the stock price moved as indicated by the line, the writer would buy the stock at Point 1, sell it at Point 2, and buy again at Point 3. It should be pointed out immediately that with reasonable decision points a stock would practically never require 3 reactions and the graph is only descriptive.

S2D

    Initial — The writer starts from a fully hedged position.

Defensive — The writer stays hedged until the option expires unless the stock moves down to a preset level in which case he sells out his stock position. He remains naked unless the stock turns and moves up to another preset level.

    Graphically the strategy is portrayed in Figure 4.2.

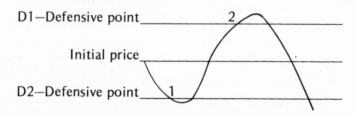

Figure 4.2. Strategy S2D — Limits

    If the stock price moved as indicated by the line, the writer sells his stock position at 1, buys again at 2, and sells at 3. As mentioned above this would be a rare occurrence and is used for descriptive purposes only.

S3D

S3D (partial hedge) is a combination of S1D and S2D. If the hedge is a half hedge then half the shares are treated as they are in S1D and half as in S2D.

LEVEL II CONSIDERATIONS

As can be seen, the major difference between Level I and Level II Strategies is the taking of a defensive position in regard to the underlying stock. The significant decision to be made is where the defensive points (D1, D2) should be set. Based on short run stock movements there seems little reason to have the up protection set further from the initial stock price than the down protection. Thus D1 and D2 will be the same distance above and below the initial stock price. D, representing D1 and D2, can be expressed in terms of a percentage change in stock price. Thus D = 10% means that an unhedged position will be covered by buying in the stock if a stock increase of 10% or more occurs and a hedged position in the stock will be sold out if the stock drops by 10% or more. 10% is not a suggested level, only an example, and the problem of setting the best level for D will be discussed later.

Note that the decision point (D) is expressed as the change in the market price of the underlying stock from its price when the option was issued and not from the striking price. There will be no difference between the two for OTC options since the striking price is usually the market price at the time of issue. Sometimes OTC options, and almost always CBOE options, are sold away from the market. In this case the striking price and the market price at writing will not be the same. In that event, which will be covered more fully under Level III Strategies, the market price at issue should be the base from which D is measured.

FACTORS INFLUENCING PROFIT

Returning to Level I Strategies it can be shown that the profitability of writing options can be expressed in terms of Expected Value (EP) as a function, f( ), of a number of variables. (It may be wise for the reader to review the definition of EP and f( ) in Chapter 1.) Under conditions of probability profit can be expressed:

$$EP = f(O,P,pD,S,M)$$

where O is the option terms — premium, length, striking price.

pD is the probability distribution of the possible prices of the underlying stock on option expiration or exercise.

S is the strategy (S1, S2, S3, S1D, etc.) employed.

P is the current price of the underlying stock.

M are the other conditions that affect profit such as margin requirements, tax and so forth. M will be ignored for the purposes here.

In making the decision to write an option, all of the variables above are known except for pD, the probability distribution for the possible prices of the stock at expiration or exercise. The programmed use of options is based on the assumption that over time and over a diverse portfolio of writing there will be an average change of 0% in the price of underlying stocks from issue to expiration. This does not mean that individual stocks are not expected to move up or down, but that over many periods the upward moves of some stocks will be offset by the downward moves of others. Even though pD is not known, an example will be used that assumes knowledge of pD to illustrate the nature of option strategies and the risks involved.

EXAMPLE – CALCULATING EXPECTED PROFITABILITY

Mr. X has the opportunity of writing calls on 200 shares of XYZ Co.

The option conditions are:

Striking price and market price of XYZ = $50

Premium 750 (per option) = $1500

Length of option 192 days

His estimates of the price of XYZ at expiration and their probabilities (pD), expressed as change from initial price of 50, is shown in Table 4.1.

Table 4.1. Probability Distribution of Changes in XYZ Stock Price

Price change (points)	Probability
+10	.1
+ 5	.2
0	.4
- 5	.2
- 10	.1

Ignoring commissions for simplicity and with all the required variables known we now calculate his stock losses for Strategy S2 in Table 4.2. Remember from Chapter One that expected loss is not Mr. X's actual loss but the average loss he could expect if he embarked on this venture a large number of times.

Table 4.2. Expected Stock Losses for XYZ (2 Options)

Possible Price changes	Probability of each change	Resulting Stock loss	Probability X loss
+10	.1	0	0
+ 5	.2	0	0
0	.4	0	0
- 5	.2	$1000	-200
- 10	.1	2000	-200
Total	1.0		-400 = Expected loss

Ignoring commissions:

Expected Profit = Premiums - Expected Stock Loss

$$1100 = 1500 - 400$$

Return on Investment assuming no use of margin

$$ROI = \frac{Profit}{Investment} \times \frac{365}{Length\ of\ option}$$

$$\frac{Expected}{ROI} = \frac{1,100}{10,000-1,500} \times \frac{365}{192} = .246 = 24.6\%$$

Note that the word "Expected" before any value means the average expectancy of that value and not its real outcome on any one occasion. If the average height of U.S. males is 70 inches, then the expected height of a randomly selected man is 70 inches. Not every man will have a height of 70 inches.

The example can also be used to examine the nature of risk in the case of a particular decision. The profit can be put in a probability table, Table 4.3.

Table 4.3
Expected Profit for XYZ (2 options)

Possible Price changes	Probability of each change	Resulting profit	Probability X profit
+10	.1	$1500	$150
+ 5	.2	1500	300
0	.4	1500	600
- 5	.2	500	100
- 10	.1	-500	- 50
Total	1.0		$1100 = Expected Profit

Table 4.3 enables direct calculation of Expected Profit and, of course, agrees with the previous calculation. The Expected Profit table also allows a view of the risks that are involved. The writer, under the circumstances in the example, can lose $500 and, in addition, the chance of this loss is .1 or 10%. The above example is not meant to be representative and generally a 15% call premium would involve a stock with a wider pD than that illustrated and thus greater risk of loss.

Once again, the pD of a stock cannot usually be determined. If it can, direct stock purchase or the speculative use of options should be considered. The programmed use of options operates on the average variability of stocks and the illustrated precise analysis is not necessary. General selection criteria to help weed out stocks with extreme risk relative to the premium can be used and these will be discussed later in this chapter.

ADDITIONAL PROFITABILITY FACTORS — LEVEL II STRATEGIES

It was pointed out that Expected Profit could be expressed as

Expected Profit = $f(O,P,pD,S)$ for Level I Strategies. For Level II Strategies this is expanded to

$$EP = f(O,P,pD,S,D,V)$$

where O is the option terms — Premium, length, striking price.

P is price of the underlying stock at issue.

pH is the probability distribution of the possible stock prices at expiration or exercise.

S is the strategy employed (S1, S2, S3, S1D, S2D, S3D).

D is the defensive decision point (i.e. $\mp$ 10%).

V is the variability of the stock.

D and V did not appear as factors in Level I Strategies, but the use of Decision Points (D) for determining when to "buy in" or "sell out" the underlying stock makes them important. The determination that must be made by the investor is — exactly where the decision point should be. This subject will be discussed later in the chapter.

"V" indicates the variability of the underlying

stock. In Level I Strategies the probability distribution (pD) of stock prices at expiration was an important determinant of profitability. Certainly the variability of the stock partially determines how widely distributed the final prices might be, but in Level II Strategies variability is even more important. Variability in this case means the likelihood that the stock will change price rapidly through time. If a stock moves up and down frequently it may move through the decision points a number of times as was shown in Figures 4.1 and 4.2.

Each time the stock reaches a decision point a defensive stock purchase or sale is required and each of these involves a realized stock loss. Since these losses will quickly exhaust the premium received, Level II Strategies will be most successful with stocks that do not have high variability.

Before examining ways of determining the variability of stocks and the setting of decision point levels, some idea of the profitability of Level II Options will be presented.

PROFITABILITY OF LEVEL II STRATEGIES

It is not, of course, possible to predict exactly the profitability of Level II Strategies. There has been only limited research on these strategies and variation in profitability will occur depending on the precise strategy and the other rules used. Following are two bases for estimating Level II profitability.

1. Boness (Reference 3), although his primary research was not in this area, did some preliminary

research on a version of strategy S1D. The results indicated an average return of 36.9% on investment for 6 month calls.

2. The author (Reference 5) conducted a study which concerned itself with testing Level I and Level II strategies under adverse conditions. While the results do not indicate average performance, they do indicate how well a diverse portfolio of options may perform under volatile market conditions. The results for the six strategies in each of 5 periods of six month duration are shown in Table 4.4.

Table 4.4
Return on Investment by Period
For Six Decision Strategies

Period	S1	S2	S3
1	.092	.064	.078
2	- .684	.348	-.168
3	-1.072	.692	-.190
4	.616	- .076	.270
5	.740	-1.452	-.356
Average	- .062	- .085	-.073

Period	S1D	S2D	S3D
1	.220	- .154	.033
2	- .092	.100	.004
3	.172	.124	.148
4	.476	- .096	.190
5	.232	- .001	.116
Average	.202	.005	.098

Stock Options

As was mentioned in the previous chapter, Level I Strategies show a loss during these volatile periods. The difference between S1 and S2 is accounted for by higher commissions in S2. Level II Strategies range from breaking even to a return of 20% under adverse conditions. Strategy S1D, on average, is best in the research partially due to fewer commissions. However strategy S3D, the half hedge position, is safest over all conditions. The returns listed assume the use of margin and include commission charges.

The results from these two studies converge on the generally held belief that option writers following a systematic and continual program average about 20% per year. However, the strategies and variations discussed in this chapter and to be discussed in the next chapter are more sophisticated than those generally in use and can be expected to perform better than past strategies.

It is the opinion of the author that the option writer using Level II strategies can expect, for any one year period, to earn a rate of return of between 5 and 40% with an average return of about 23% assuming the following conditions:

1. The writer utilizes the safest strategy, S3D.

2. The writer analyzes the decision elements described in the next section of this chapter.

3. The writer maintains a diverse portfolio of writing. Such diversity will require a minimum of $15,000 invested in option.

4. The writer diversifies his writing through time so unusual market conditions will affect only part of his portfolio.

SELECTING STOCKS FOR WRITING

As previously indicated it is not generaly possible to predict, even probabilistically, how a stock may behave over the option exercise period. Several methods have been developed, however, for rejecting stocks that are too volatile and thereby have low profit potential. The previously cited study by the author (Reference 5) indicated that profitability could be increased by eliminating low priced stocks which appear to have greater volatility. The best cut off point was $16 and profits were greatest when options were not written on stocks with prices of $16 or less even though the percentage premium may be higher.

Another interesting outcome of the research was the finding that higher yields do not necessarily come from writing on stocks with higher premiums. There appears to be, as might be expected, a relationship between the premium paid and the likelihood that the stock will be volatile and thus risky. The study did indicate that it is not generally wise to accept premiums of less than 12% (6 months options) because of the transaction costs, but this was based on a fairly speculative portfolio and 10% is likely a good minimum level.

Since the profit potential of writing options is related positively to the size of the premium and negatively to the degree of risk from price variation, a selection process should include consideration of both. The variability of a stock can be estimated by its past performance. This is accomplished by examining the past record of the stock and seeing in what percentage of the time it has made moves that would reduce the profitability of option writing or generate a loss. The rating on variability given the stock can then be compared to the premium to establish an index of profitability for each stock that is being considered as a writing possibility. This procedure can be approximated by looking at charts and even a rough estimate should greatly increase the writers chance of success. Such information calculated by computer on a weekly basis for listed options is also available from Quantitative Decision Systems, Inc. in their Stock Option Writers Service (Reference 1).

It must be emphasized that the writer usually cannot get satisfactory premiums if he simply selects a few stocks he would like to write on. He must look at those stocks for which options are in demand, particularly those listed on the CBOE, and select from among the opportunities.

DEFENSIVE DECISION POINT (D)

Strategies Level II require a set defensive decision point where naked positions will be covered and hedged positions closed out. The short term variability of stocks makes decision points too close to the initial price impractical and decision points too far from the initial price may absorb too much loss. The study by the author (Reference 5) indicated $\mp$ 15% was the optimum level for the stocks written and for the periods of time tested. Since the stocks in that study were fairly speculative, lower limits might be better on average. Calculation of the best level for D can be determined by ongoing research, but overall it appears D should be no less than ∓ 9% nor more than ∓ 15%. Using 12% as a preliminary estimate, Strategies Level II would put an "up stop" at 12% above all naked positions and a "stop loss" at 12% below all hedged positions. These stop orders should be placed with the broker when the options are written. The investor should not depend on his ability to implement Level II Strategies by following the newspapers.

SUMMARY

It is the author's opinion that option writers using Level II Strategies and taking the precautions recommended can realize an average return on investment of over 20% per year even without a great deal of analysis of individual stocks. If listed options are used the suggestions for "away from the market" calculations in the next chapter should be read. The other aspects of Level III Strategies are not necessary but do offer additional opportunities. While 20% per year may not be attractive to speculators it is an extremely high rate of return and will double capital every 4 years.

CHAPTER FIVE

CALL OPTIONS — LEVEL III STRATEGIES

Level II Strategies have been rather extensively developed and are recommended for OTC option writing. Level III Strategies deal with the additional problems and opportunities brought about by options listed on the Chicago Board Options Exchange. The following differences are important:

1. CBOE options have standardized striking prices. That means that all options of the same class will have the same striking price (i.e. $40). If a stock has moved substantially since trading in the option began, a new class of options in that stock may be started (i.e. $50), but there will be many options with the same striking price and they are interchangeable. This contrasts to OTC options where every option is unique.

2. CBOE options have standardized expiration dates. There are several dates (last day of January, April, July, October) but all options of the same class and the same date are identical. Only three dates will be traded at any one time for each class of option on a particular security.

3. The standardized striking price may never coincide precisely with the market price of the stock when an option is written. The premium then, allows for the option being "away from the market." Options "in the money" will have higher premiums than normal and those "out of the money" will have

lower than normal premiums.

4. While a writer of an OTC option must be ready to deliver the stock at the request of the buyer until the option expiration date, the listed writer can terminate his position by "buying back" the option he sold. Likewise the buyer of an OTC option can only exercise or not exercise his option, the listed option buyer may sell his option on the secondary market. This is possible because of the standardization of option terms.

Anyone familiar with commodities trading can see the similarity between listed options and commodities, but there are differences in respect to exercise since the commodity contract is a purchase agreement and the option is an option, not binding on the buyer. It is the nature of an option that the buyer's loss is limited to the amount paid for the option. This is not true of the margin deposited by a commodity buyer. There are also options on unregulated commodities but these will not be discussed.

The principal strategy differences between OTC and listed options are:

1. Consideration of the effect of "away from the market" transactions, and

2. The potential use of options to hedge options or "spreading."

These differences will be discussed below.

AWAY FROM THE MARKET

Consider an option on XYZ corporation whose

stock is selling at $40. Suppose that the option is listed at a striking price of $40 (the market price) and on the first day trades at $6 (on the CBOE premiums are expressed per share even though 100 share lots are the basic unit). Suppose further that the next day XYZ is selling at $45 a share. What should be the premium then. Forgetting the fact that one day has elapsed; it can be assumed that a call on XYZ is worth $6, but now the option is $5 into the money as well as being a call on the stock for its remaining life. Should the option now be worth $11? No, because to realize the gain on the stock the owner of the option would have to exercise and thereby give up the call value. On average it could be expected that the $5 would not be lost, but there is risk involved in buying and holding this $5 gain and so buyers will generally pay only a portion of the temporary gain. What portion is not determinable. The history of the small portion of OTC stocks that are sold on a secondary basis indicates that generally the option will go up ½ of the amount it is in the money. If that held true XYZ 40's would sell at 8½.

It is difficult to analyze the proportion paid for options in the money. Part of this difficulty comes from lack of historical data, but it also results from the inability to determine what the call portion is worth. In the XYZ company the option might climb more than would be indicated by the amount it is in the money because the stock is now "hotter" and the option commands a higher premium.

On the other side of the coin is the option that

is "out of the money". Suppose an ABC option has a striking price of $30 and ABC is now at $25. Also suppose that yesterday ABC was $30 and the option was selling at 4. The rule of thumb on OTC special offerings was ½ for "in the money" and also is ½ for "out of the money" so the price on the options might be 1½ with ABC at $25. There is a limit in this rule since if ABC stock went to $20, it would indicate an option value of -1 which is not possible. Unexpired options usually have some value, even far out of the money, until they expire.

Perhaps it is more appropriate to consider what portion of the "in the money" amount should be acceptable to the writer of an option rather than what typical transactions are. Since the writer is, in a sense, giving a bonus to the buyer when an option is in the money, he must be concerned about whether the offsetting premium increase is sufficient. Listed options come into existence with an expiration date approximately 9 months in the future. It is the author's feeling, based on what must be limited analysis, that the writer should expect to receive about 50% of the "in the money" amount in addition to the required premium for the call values at the beginning of the 9 month option period. This per cent should increase steadily to 95% at the expiration date. At the same time, however, the call value is decreasing from its maximum value at 9 months to 0 at expiration. The writer should look for opportunities where the combined premium for call value and "being in the money" is disproportionally high.

Before assessing the amount of premium being received for the risk in writing, the writer should subtract an estimate of the amount being received for the option being "in the money."

While there are disadvantages to writing "in the money" there is one significant advantage. The payment for the "in the money" portion of the premium is paid to the writer immediately and reduces the amount of investment needed for the writing position. It is not generally recommended that options considerably out of the money be written even though the risk is reduced, since the investment base is higher and transaction costs use up the reduced premium. Once again, however, there can be opportunities if the market does not discount the premiums as much as it should. These relationships will be examined at greater length in the next section.

EVALUATING THE PREMIUM

This section considers a methodology for evaluating a premium for its potential profitability. This is done in several steps.

STEP 1 — Change the premium to its % by dividing the premium by the market price of the underlying stock.

$$\text{Premium \%} = \frac{\text{Premium}}{\text{Current Market Price}}$$

Example:

XYZ Oct-40. Market price of stock $42.
Premium 7.

$$\text{Premium \%} = \frac{7}{42} = 16.7\%$$

STEP 2 — Adjust the premium to standard form by eliminating the part that is due to the option being "in the money." The suggested adjustment rates are shown in Table 5.1.

Table 5.1
Adjustment of
"In the Money" by Remaining Option Time

Months remaining	9	8	7	6	5	4	3	2	1	0
% of "in the money" to be deducted for standardizing premium	50	55	60	65	70	75	80	85	90	95

Example:

The option has a striking price of 40 so at a market price of 42 the option is 2 points in the money. If the date is July 1, the option has 4 months left in the exercise period and Table 5.1 indicates 75%. This means the writer should

62

expect that 75% of the in the money amount or 1½ points should be deducted from the premium to arrive at the portion being paid for the call value, This gives an adjusted premium of 5½ or

$$\frac{5\frac{1}{2}}{42} = 13.1\%$$

The adjusted premium percentage indicates that the option in question is the equivalent of an option with a striking price of 42 and a premium of 5½.

STEP 3 — Before the possible return on investment can be estimated, it is necessary to allow for the transaction costs involved in writing. This cost may be the same regardless of the length of the option and this accounts for the fact that 6 month calls do not cost twice as much as 3 month calls. The actual transaction cost can vary depending on strategy and the number of calls written, but it is the author's feeling that 4% (of the stock cost) should be subtracted from the option yield.

Example:
The adjusted option yield of 13.1% is adjusted to:

$$13.1\% - 4\% = 9.1\%$$

STEP 4 — Evaluation of the option return. The potential yield of the option should be calculated on a monthly basis so that comparisons can be made between options and then a decision made as to the attractiveness of the yields.

Example:

The final yield was estimated at 9.1% and the remaining time, in months, is 4. This gives a monthly return of:

$$9.1\% \div 4 = 2.28\%$$

This would be a high yield with the usual range being between 1% and 2% per month. The use of margin will approximately double the yield and it can be seen that 1—2% a month provides a potential yield of 24—48% a year. While it is suggested that a potential yield of less that 1% not be written, the desirability of a potential yield can only be determined relative to the risk.

Risk can be evaluated in two ways. The simplest is to choose a number of possible writes on stocks that are perceived to offer about equal risk and to write on those that offer the highest potential yield.

Another approach is to rate stocks for risk and compare potential yield to the risk rating. The rating of risk can be accomplished as previously described by a general review of the stock's past performance or by an analytical determination of movement probabilities and variability. For the individual desiring as analytical an evaluation as possible but not wishing to do the analysis such a service is available (Reference 1).

The elements of a professional call writing strategy have now been covered. Suggestions for the inexperienced writer are as follows.

1. Have at least $15,000 for your call writing portfolio.

2. Diversify your writings. With the minimum working capital write only 2 calls on any one stock.

3. Distribute your writing through time. If writing 6 month OTC options, one-sixth of the calls should be written each month. On the CBOE have one-fourth of your money in each of the four standard exercise dates.

4. Use strategy S3D, the half hedge, unless you are strongly bullish (S2D) or strongly bearish (S1D) on the market. An alternative to using S3D is to use S1D on some writing and S2D on the rest.

5. Use ∓ 12% as your defensive point initially. It can be adjusted over time based on your experience. Put stop orders in when you write. Do not depend on reading the paper and reacting.

6. Use a broker that is familiar with options and whose margin requirements correspond closely to the NYSE or CBOE requirements listed in the final chapter.

7. Compare writing opportunities carefully. Put CBOE options into standard form by adjusting for "in the money." Subtract 4% from the potential yield to allow for administrative costs. Calculate the

potential monthly yield. Compare this yield to that of options on similar stocks or compare the yield to the variability of the stock and choose the best opportunities. Do not accept potential yields of less than 1% a month, since even very stable stocks may involve stock losses.

8. Evaluate your results, but to be fair, they must be evaluated over a reasonable period of time.

While the material covered so far should be sufficient to enable the reader to begin on an option writing program, the next section covers two additional opportunities available with CBOE options — Hedging with options and option defensive strategies.

HEDGING OPTIONS WITH OPTIONS

As was pointed out earlier, CBOE options share with commodity contracts the standardization of exercise dates. In the case of CBOE options these dates are the last day of January, April, July, and October. As in the case of commodities a number of these expiration dates will be trading at the same time. This permits the hedging of one option with another or as it has been called in commodities "spreading." The use of the spread can best be explained with an example.

Suppose, on the CBOE, July, October and January options are trading and on May 1 the prices of these options for XYZ company are:

		Option Price	Stock Price
XYZ	July - 40	4	40
XYZ	Oct-40	5	40
XYZ	Jan-40	6	40

A spread position can be taken by Buying XYZ Jan-40 and Selling XYZ July-40. The cost is:

$$\begin{array}{lr} \text{Pay } 600 + 25 \text{ (commission)} & -625 \\ \text{Receive } 400 - 25 & +375 \\ \hline & -250 \end{array}$$

First, the results if XYZ remains at about 40 through October, will be examined. Based on the above premiums if XYZ stays at 40, on August 1, the options will have the following values:

XYZ	July-40	0 (expired)
XYZ	Oct-40	4
XYZ	Jan-40	5

Since the July option has expired the writer can now write an XYZ-Oct-40 and receive:

$$400 - 25 = \$375$$

If XYZ stays at 40, on November 1 the Oct-40 option will expire and the writer can now sell the January option, which should be selling at 4, for:

$$400 - 25 = \$375$$

67

Stock Options

In all, the writer will have paid $625 and received $375 + $375 + $375 for a net profit of

$$1125 - 625 = \$500$$

Using the CBOE margin requirements (Chapter 8) the investment would be $650 and the annual return on investment would be:

$$\frac{500}{650} \times 2 = 154\%$$

A profit of $500 would only occur, however, if the optioned stock stayed at approximately the same price. This would be an unusual occurrence and $500 represents the maximum profit. Based on the assumptions in this example, it might be expected that, if the stock moved up significantly during May, June, or July, the prices at the end of July might appear as follows:

		Option price	Stock price
XYZ	July-40	10	50
XYZ	Oct-40	11½	50
XYZ	Jan-40	13½	50

The writer can liquidate his position by "buying back" the July option and selling the January option. This will yield:

$$375 + 1325 - 625 - 1025 = \$50 \text{ profit (for 3 months)}$$

The writer can also continue his position by "buying back" the July option and writing an October option. In this case the calculation must continue based on assumptions about XYZ stock performance.

XYZ might also go down substantially during the period of the July option. If this occurs it might be expected that prices at the end of July would appear as follows.

		Option Price	Stock Price
XYZ	July-40	0	30
XYZ	Oct-40	1¼	30
XYZ	Jan-40	2½	30

The writer in this case would let the July option expire and write an October option receiving $125-25. If the stock remains down, the January option would be worth 1¼ after the October option expires and so upon selling it the writer would receive an additional $125-25. The transaction summary now is:

375 + 100 + 100 - 625 = -$50 loss (for 6 months)

The figures in the example are illustrative only, but the reader can see that such a spread offers the writer the opportunity for a gain of up to $500 and the risk of loss of only $50. No matter what happens the maximum loss will be approximately $250. This would be a very attractive spread opportunity. The attractiveness of the opportunity was determined by the relative prices of the 3 XYZ options and such opportunities do not appear all of the time. The professional writer, however, should be alert for discrepancies in the prices of options on the same stock and take advantage of spread opportunities if they occur.

DEFENSIVE STRATEGIES WITH OPTIONS

Strategies Level II required that defensive steps be taken in the stocks when options are written. For example, in strategy S1D the option would be written naked but the writer would buy the stock if it went up by 12%. An alternative to this is to buy back the option and liquidate the position. This approach is most appealing if the writer feels he has written on a stock that now appears to have become extremely volatile — up and down. An example will enable the reader to follow this approach.

Suppose the writer has written an option, XYZ Oct-50, on May 1 for a premium of $750. At the time the stock was selling at 50. The writer wrote naked and, following the 12% decision point, will buy the stock if it goes up 12% (reaches 56). Two months later the stock has risen gradually to 55½ and the October option is now selling for 9½. Following strategy S1D the writer will buy in at 56. But if the writer feels XYZ may go up and then down and perhaps up again because it has become a volatile issue, he can liquidate his position by buying back his call at 9½. The transaction summary, subtracting commissions, will then be:

$$725 - 975 = -250 \text{ (loss)}$$

While a $250 loss is certainly not desirable the writing position was taken with the possibility of a $725 gain. Sometimes it is better to say "this is one of the bad ones," and close the position. The ordinary approach of S1D would be to buy the stock which will still give the writer a chance for a $100 gain if the stock stays above 50. If the stock goes below 50, however, there will be a loss. The position should be closed out if the writer feels the volatility of the stock has changed and the option is now too great of a risk.

CLOSING OUT PROFITS

One last variation of strategy is the closing out of a position to take a profit. Suppose an option with a 6 month remaining duration was written naked for a premium of $600. If the stock has dropped considerably in three months and the option price is now 2, the writer may feel that an additional $200 profit for three months is too low and buy back the option thereby realizing his $(600 - 25) - (200 + 25) =$ $350 profit for the three expired months.

This alternative should be considered whenever a stock moves quickly. The return that remains to be made on a position should continually be compared to the potential return available on new positions, so that such positions can be cleared out when most of their profit has been realized.

Closing out may also be advantageous in spreads. A spread was recommended when two options on the same stock with different expiration dates were very close in price. It may not be necessary to wait until the near term option expires since the market may recognize that the two options are too close in price and they may separate. If this occurs the spreader may realize his profits quickly.

For example, suppose the writer has bought XYZ-Jan at 5 and sold XYZ-Jul at 3½. If the price changes to XYZ-Jul at 3 and XYZ-Jan at 6½, the position can be liquidated by buying back July and selling January. This gives an immediate profit of:

$$(350 - 300) + (650 - 500) = \$200$$
$$\text{(excluding commissions)}$$

This chapter concludes the analysis of option writing as a programmed investment technique. The next two chapters will consider the speculative use of options and the final chapter will discuss tax implications and margin requirements.

CHAPTER SIX
CALL OPTIONS — SPECULATIVE STRATEGIES

As defined in Chapter One, speculation in the stock market involves the attempt to predict and take advantage of short term movements in the market or in individual issues. Short term can refer to any period of time, but arbitrarily a two year period can be set. Since options only run to 9 months or a year at most, efforts to make profits on options by predicting stock movements must be considered short term and therefore speculative.

Speculative does not mean that options are more risky than common stocks. The use of call options in lieu of buying the underlying stock can be more or less risky than stock purchase depending on the approach taken.

While, unlike a programmed approach, the speculative use of options depends largely on the judgement of the investor, there are analytical steps that can be taken to help the investor make better decisions. These partial strategies will be discussed following description of the various ways that the investor can use call options.

BUYING STOCK

In order to examine the use of calls it is desirable to compare such uses with the obvious alternative of buying the stock. Since the call buyer, in addition to other objectives to be discussed, is generally looking for leverage, calls will be compared to buying stock on margin. Margin requirements are continually varied as a stabilizing factor so an average margin requirement of 60% will be used. The interest charge for margin money will be ½% per month. This may be a little low but it will serve for illustration purpose.

Suppose an investor feels that XYZ stock is underpriced and will move up significantly in the next half year. XYZ is selling at $50 a share and the investor buys 100 shares paying approximately $3000 and margining the remaining $2000. If the possibilities that can occur are reduced to 5 for illustration purposes, it is possible to examine (Table 6.1) the outcomes for the stock purchase at the end of 6 months.

Table 6.1 Outcomes for XYZ Stock Purchase

Possible stock change	Profit (after transaction costs)	% return on investment ($3000 annualized)
+20 pts.	$1810	+120.6%
+10	810	+ 54.0
0	- 190	- 12.6
- 10	- 1183	- 78.9
- 20	- 2174	- 144.9

As stated, the example is illustrative and extreme values are shown to demonstrate possible outcomes even though these extreme values might occur only rarely.

BUYING CALLS — RISK PROTECTION

The call can be used to limit downside risk. When calls are used this way the same number of shares are optioned as could have been bought on margin. Carrying the same example further and assuming the cost of a 6 month call on XYZ to be $750, the investor would buy a call on 100 shares of XYZ with a striking price of $50. The same possible stock outcomes and their profit results follow in Table 6.2.

Table 6.2
Outcomes for XYZ Option Purchase
(Risk Limiting)

Possible stock change	Profit (after transaction costs)	% return on investment ($775 annualized)
+20 pts.	$1200	+309.7%
+10	200	+ 51.6
0	- 775	- 200.0
- 10	- 775	- 200.0
- 20	- 775	- 200.0

The effect of the option is to limit the loss to $775. At lower level increases in the stock the option will not produce as much profit as the stock purchase but as the amount of gain increases the option profit moves up rapidly. If the investor wishes to limit loss the alternative of optioning an equal number of shares is very attractive. The cost of this protection is greater losses or lower profits if the stock moves up only slightly. This approach seems best when the investor feels the stock will either move up substantially or go down.

BUYING CALLS — MAXIMUM LEVERAGE

Under the risk protection approach the call buyer optioned the same number of shares he would have bought in an outright purchase (100 in our example). In the leverage maximizing approach the buyer invests an *equal amount of money.*

In the stock example the investor put up $3000 plus commissions for 100 shares of XYZ on margin. With this investment he can, alternatively, buy calls on 400 shares. If he chooses this approach the previously considered stock changes will yield the results in Table 6.3.

Table 6.3
Outcomes for XYZ Option Purchase
(High Leverage)

Possible stock change	Profit (after transaction costs)	% return on investment ($3050 annualized)
+20 pts.	$4900	+321.3%
+10	900	+ 59.0
0	- 3050	- 200.0
- 10	- 3050	- 200.0
- 20	- 3050	- 200.0

As can be seen, the objective of higher leverage is achieved. If the stock moves up substantially the profits will be considerably higher for the option purchase than for purchase of the stock. It should be noted well that if the stock stays the same or goes down the entire investment is lost.

The choice of alternatives clearly depends on the investor's estimate of what will happen. This estimate is one of judgment, but later in the chapter some techniques for assisting the investor's judgment will be presented.

WRITING CALLS FOR SPECULATION

Earlier chapters emphasized call writing as the basic ingredient in a programmed investment approach. It is possible to use call writing speculatively, however, as a substitute for going short the stock. Most frequently a put, as will be discussed in the next chapter, is used as a substitute for going short, but a naked call can be used to reduce the risk of a short position at the cost of limiting potential profits.

If the investor in our previous example of XYZ Corporation is bearish on the stock, the most obvious strategy is to go short. The results from shorting the stock and writing a naked call will be different in the following respects.

1. The naked call writer will have the same losses as the stock shorter if the stock moves up, except that the call writer will have an additional $750, the call premium.

2. If the stock moves down the naked call writer

will have $750 more profit than the stock shorter except that the maximum profit is $750.

In summary, the naked call writer will do $750 better than the stock shorter and for this bonus limits his maximum gain to $750. The % return on investment may be different for the two approaches since the margin requirements on a naked call are usually lower than the requirements for a short position.

ANALYSIS IN THE SPECULATIVE USE OF CALLS

To make a profit from the purchase of a call it is necessary not only to choose a stock that will go up, but to choose one that will go up by more than the amount of the premium paid. The various theories and analytical devices available for predicting those stocks most likely to increase will not be discussed here since they are the same as would be used without options. There is an additional device, however, that may help the call buyer determine whether or not a stock is a good option candidate and that is the "stock variability" which was discussed as part of call writing strategies.

While the programmed call writer is looking for stocks that have low variability (variability is the characteristic of a stock that makes it move, up or down, by a large percentage) or at least low variability in relationship to its option premium, the call buyer is looking for stocks that have high variability. As mentioned previously variability can be assessed, at least partially, by looking at charts of past performance and estimating those stocks that have a history of big moves. The estimate of variability on a historic basis can also be accomplished by detailed analysis of prior movements and the frequency with which these movements exceed the typical premium level (Reference 1).

In summary it can be seen that for short term profit objectives the call option is an interesting alternative to stock purchase. The risk reducing use of options, the leverage seeking use of options, and the purchase of the stock all offer different outcomes in a particular situation and the choices for the bullish investor must depend on his estimate of the future. Additionally, naked call writing can be used speculatively as an occasional substitute for selling short.

CHAPTER SEVEN
PUT OPTIONS — SPECULATIVE STRATEGIES

To a large extent the speculative use of puts is merely the opposite of what was presented in Chapter Six. There are some noteworthy differences, however, which will be discussed in this chapter. In addition, the purposes of buying straddles (a put and a call) will be examined. The major use of puts is as an alternative to selling short. As in the previous chapter, the analysis of the option strategies must begin by reviewing the non-option alternative. It should be noted that at the time of publication puts are not traded on the CBOE (although they are planned) and calculations assume use of OTC puts.

SHORTING STOCK

Selling short is simply selling a stock prior to purchasing on the expectation that the stock is going down and can be bought later at a price lower than the selling price. The technical aspects of how brokers arrange this rather unusual transaction will not be covered here. For comparison an example of a short sale will be developed. The same example as in the previous chapter will be followed.

An investor feels that XYZ stock will go down in price during the next six months. XYZ is selling at $50 a share and the investor sells short 100 shares, putting up 60% of market value or $3000. Considering five possibilities that can occur, the five profit results are shown in Table 7.1.

Table 7.1
Outcomes for XYZ Stock Short Sale

Possible stock change	Profit (after transaction costs)	% return on investment ($3000 annualized)
+20 pts.	$-2190	- 146.0%
+10	-1190	- 79.3
0	- 190	- 12.7
- 10	817	+ 54.5
- 20	1826	+121.7

As in the Chapter 6 example, extreme values are used to illustrate outcomes and should not be construed as ordinary.

BUYING PUTS – RISK PROTECTION

The put can be used to limit upside risk when the investor wishes to take a short position. When puts are used this way a put is purchased for the *same number of shares* as could have been sold short. The results for possible outcomes in the XYZ example are shown in Table 7.2. It is assumed the price of a 6 month put is $450. Puts generally sell for ½ to ¾ the price of a call.

Table 7.2
Outcomes of XYZ Put Purchase
(Risk Limiting)

Possible stock change	Profit (after transaction costs)	% return on investment ($450 annualized)
+20 pts.	$- 450	- 200.0%
+10	- 450	- 200.0
0	- 450	- 200.0
- 10	434	+192.9
- 20	1433	+636.9

As can be seen the option limits the loss to $450, the price of the option, as compared to a possible loss of $2190 in the case of a short sale. On the other hand, profit, particularly for a small downward move in the stock, is reduced. This approach seems best when the investor feels the stock will either fall dramatically or move up a bit. If only a moderate downward move is expected a short sale will be better.

BUYING PUTS — MAXIMUM LEVERAGE

Under the risk protection policy the investor bought puts on the same number of shares he could have sold short. Using the maximum leverage strategy the buyer invests the *same amount of money* he would have used for selling short. On this basis the put buyer can buy approximately 7 puts. His investment is $3150. The results for the outcomes in the XYZ example are shown in Table 7.3.

Table 7.3
Outcomes of XYZ Put Purchase
(High Leverage)

Possible stock change	Profit (after transaction costs)	% return on investment ($3150 annualized)
+20 pts.	$- 3150	- 200.0%
+10	- 3150	- 200.0
0	- 3150	- 200.0
- 10	2874	+182.5
- 20	10,300	+654.0

Both profit and loss are greater under this strategy than when the stock is sold short, so the object of greater leverage is achieved. Even though the potential profits are extremely high, the investor will loose his entire investment if the stock stays the same or moves up. The advisability of this approach depends on the confidence the investor has in his prediction that the stock will fall significantly.

There is another significant difference between buying puts and shorting the stock. All short sales are considered short term gains for tax purposes no matter how long the position is maintained. In the case of a put, if it is purchased and sold back to the broker for its value after 6 months have elapsed, it is a long term gain and taxed at a lower rate. This tax advantage for bearish investors makes the put even more desirable as an alternative to selling short.

ANALYSIS OF THE SPECULATIVE USE OF PUTS

As in the use of calls the profitability of puts depends not only on knowing which stocks will make a move, but on knowing that the movements will be substantial enough to justify the amount of the premium. Once again analysis of stocks can indicate variability and isolate those stocks that tend to make large moves. Puts are lower priced than calls and therefore offer greater profit potential for equivalent moves in the underlying stock. The general feeling is that the long term trend is bullish and thus there always seems to be greater interest in calls. It is a noteworthy observation that the difference in price between puts and calls is, on average, 5% on the underlying stock or an annualized percentage of 10%. This more than compensates for the long range growth trend and the wise speculator should be alert to put opportunities when he is bearish on a stock or on the market.

STRADDLES

A Straddle is a put and a call on the same stock with the same terms. Early in this book it was pointed out that the put generally was not a good write, but because of the unusual margin treatment given to straddles investors often will write them. Most often a written straddle is split and the call and put sold separately to different buyers. Sometimes the put is converted, as explained previously, into a call. Under certain conditions, however, the straddle can be bought for speculative purposes. Rarely could a buyer expect to see a stock vary enough so that both the put and call could be exercised profitably. To be profitable then, one side must be profitable enough to defray the cost of the total premium which, for a six month straddle, might be 20%. If the buyer was bullish or bearish he would buy either a put or a call and save premium, so the only situation that makes sense for the straddle buyer is one where he feels the stock will make a dramatic move but the direction is not known. While this is not a common situation, it does occur. For example, a company rumored to have made a technical breakthrough might be a good candidate. If the stock previously sold at 30 and expectation of the new development has pushed the stock to 60, a straddle buyer might estimate that comfirmation of the development would push the stock to 100 and failure would see it go back to 30. Bausch & Lomb and National Patent were in this type of position during 1972. There have been cases where a "buy out" at a substantial premium has been in the offing and during the negotiations the stock has partially reflected the anticipated tender price. A straddle might show a profit regardless of the final decision, since failure of the proposed merger would push the stock back to its original level or lower and success would push the stock up further.

In summary, puts can be effective speculative tools. In addition to the advantages of calls there are some tax advantages over going short the stock. The combined put and call, the straddle, also has some uses, but they are more rare. All the risks and limitations pointed out for calls also pertain to puts.

CHAPTER EIGHT
TAX AND MARGIN CONSIDERATIONS

An important aspect of option writing or buying is the tax consequences of transactions. Likewise the margin regulations will have a dramatic effect on the profitability of programmed call writing. This chapter will discuss these two important subjects, but two notes of caution must be interjected.

1. Both tax and margin regulations are subject to change and the investor must keep himself posted in respect to any change.

2. The interpretations given here are based on the general operating assumptions described by brokerage houses. Particularly in the case of tax matters the individual must assume the responsibility of clearing his treatment of option profits and losses with an attorney or accountant familiar with current tax rulings.

TAX TREATMENT

Buyers of Options. An option is considered a capital asset. Thus if an option is bought and sold it provides a capital gain or loss — long term if held for more than 6 months, short term if held for less. This applies to a put as well as to a call. If an option expires unexercised it is considered sold at a price of 0 and the loss is a capital loss. If an individual buys a 6 month 10 day (or longer) option and it is obvious that it will be worthless at expiration, some brokerage firms will buy it back for a token amount just before the six month period elapses so that a short term loss can be taken. Likewise, if the individual has purchased a call and the stock has moved up by the exercise date (or the reverse for a put) there will be a profit in exercising the option. However if the option is exercised and the stock position liquidated, there will be a short term gain. If the option has been held for 6 months it can be sold to the broker for the amount of profit it can generate, less a round trip commission for the stock. A profitable option should only be exercised if the investor contemplates holding the stock for more than six months because the holding period for the stock does not begin as of the purchase of the option but as of the exercise date. If an option is exercised, the premium paid can be added to the purchase price of the stock if a call, or deducted from the sale price if a put.

Writers of Options. If a put or call option expires unexercised the premium received is ordinary income on the date the option expires. If a put option is exercised the premium received by the writer reduces the cost of the securities that the writer is required to purchase. There is no taxable income until he sells the securities put to him. If a call option is exercised, the premium received by the writer is added to the proceeds of the sale. The gain is long term or short term depending on how long he has held the stock delivered.

In the latter case of an exercised call there is a

strategy that can be employed by the writer to realize a long term gain that would otherwise be short term. If the writer purchased stock and sold a call and 5½ months later the call is exercised, the writer could purchase additional stock and instruct his broker to deliver this stock against the option. Assuming the stock holds its price for the remaining two weeks he can then sell the original stock for a capital gain. He then has a long term gain and a short term loss. An example of this procedure ignoring commissions for the sake of simplicity follows.

Example: A writer buys 100 shares of XYZ at $50 per share and writes a 6 month 10 day call for $650. Five and one-half months later the stock is selling at $70 and the buyer of the call exercises.
Ordinary result: The writer delivers the 100 shares of stock.

Purchase price	$5000
Sales Price	5650
Profit	$ 650 (short term capital gain)

Alternative result: The writer buys an additional 100 shares at the market price of $7000 and delivers them against the option.

Purchase Price	$7000
Sales Price	5650
Loss	$1350 (short term capital loss)

Two weeks later he sells the original shares at the market price (assumed to still be 70).

Purchase Price	$5000
Sales Price	7000
Profit	$2000 (Long term capital gain)

Even though there will be an extra commission the tax advantage of the latter approach will outweigh this cost.

A note of caution is necessary in utilizing the alternative approach. While it is currently being used there is no definitive ruling by the Internal Revenue Service or the courts and it may be disallowed in the future. The same conditions can be accomplished, however, if the original hedge is accomplished with a convertible security or a warrant and delivery upon exercise carried out by purchase of the common stock optioned.

Straddles are generally treated as a separate put and call, but two points are important.

1. It is necessary to divide the premium received and allocate a portion to each side. This can be based on the market price of puts and calls at the time the straddle is written or the Internal Revenue Service will allow an assignment of 55% to the call and 45% to the put.

2. There is an advantage to the straddle writer that would not pertain to writing a separate put and call. If one side of the option is exercised the unexercised portion may be taken as a capital gain

rather than as ordinary income. This will prove advantageous to those investors having excess capital losses.

MARGIN REQUIREMENTS

Option Buyers. The full price of the option must be paid immediately. Unlike a stock purchase an option purchase is a cash sale and the money must be in the investor's account when the purchase is made. Brokers may permit an order to be entered if the buyer agrees to make payment the same day. These rules are the same for OTC and CBOE transactions.

Option Writers. The rules of the CBOE and New York Stock Exchange (NYSE firms must endorse OTC options) are not the same. Both regulations will be presented but it is important to note that if a CBOE option is written through a broker who is a member of the NYSE, the broker may impose the NYSE regulations on a CBOE transaction. Brokers may also have more stringent regulations than those required by either Exchange. This will be discussed more fully later.

NEW YORK STOCK EXCHANGE REGULATIONS

The following regulations are a summary of pertinent requirements. A complete set of rules can be obtained from a NYSE broker. The Federal Reserve Board changes the margin requirements on stock purchases with moderate frequency so the term "full margin" will be used instead of a specific figure to indicate the margin requirements for stock purchase. "Full margin" at this writing is 65% on stocks.

1. If a writing position is hedged with stock (long for a call and short for a put) full margin must be maintained for the stock position. The premium is received immediately and will count towards the margin requirement. No additional margin is required for the option.

2. If an option is written naked, 30% of the market value of the underlying stock must be maintained in the margin account. Generally, brokers will require that this be "marked to market." (If the stock moves up in the case of a call or down in the case of a put additional margin will be required.)

3. In the case of a straddle where the call side is hedged with stock, only an additional 25% of market price will be required as margin for the put.

4. A call is considered hedged and no additional margin is required if the writer is long a security convertible into the underlying stock. This includes warrants (even though a payment may be required for conversion), convertible bonds, and convertible preferred stocks. It is still a matter of debate as to whether ownership of an option can be used as a hedge against writing an option. Hopefully this will be decided in the near future. It is extremely important for the "spreading" strategies previously described.

CHICAGO BOARD OPTIONS EXCHANGE

The CBOE regulations are similar to the NYSE when the option is hedged by ownership of the stock. In other cases the rules are different.

1. Naked options must be covered by 100% of the market value *of the option* or a minimum of $250. This requirement is "marked to market" daily, based on the current premium of the option.

2. If an option is hedged by ownership of a security convertible into the underlying stock, in this case *including a CBOE Option,* an additional margin is required equal to 10% of the market value of the option or the underlying stock—whichever is greater. This margin is also marked to market.

BROKER REQUIREMENT

As previously indicated a broker who is a member of the NYSE may use NYSE regulations even in respect to CBOE options. Hopefully the major differences will disappear before long.

Brokers may also be more stringent in their requirements than the NYSE or CBOE. Typical additional requirements are:

1. A minimum equity for all writing or a minimum equity for naked positions.

2. Higher margin requirements for naked positions.

3. Requiring an investor writing naked to put in stop orders.

4. A limit on the proportion of writing done on a naked basis.

5. A prohibition on the naked writing of calls. Some brokers have this prohibition for occasional writers but will permit naked writing for accounts following a program of writing.

While it is reasonable to expect brokers, who must guarantee to fulfill option contracts, to protect themselves, some restrictions show a lack of regard for customers. Brokerage is a competitive business and the option writer should shop for brokerage houses that provide the best combination of service and margin rules. In no case should a writer consider doing option business with a broker who demands he stay long the stock during the entire option period. There is no reason that a writer should place himself in a position where he may be forced to watch the stock he is holding go down and down without being able to sell, nor should he be forced to make an offsetting short sale and pay the extra commissions on the whim of a broker.

A good broker is important to the option writer. If you are looking for a broker, find one that is knowledgeable regarding options. If you are in doubt as to whether he is knowledgeable, ask him how a put is converted. If you live in a large city, try and pick a brokerage firm that has an option specialist in the office. When calling a new firm don't ask the switchboard operator to speak to someone about opening an account, but ask for the sales manager and then ask him which of the registered representatives specializes in options or, better yet, go to the firm and see if the man who speaks to you is involved in options.

If you have been working with a registered representative in whom you have confidence, tell him honestly that you are interested in developing an option writing program. If he is interested in such business he can become knowledgeable fairly quickly. If he prefers not to handle options he will tell you who the option specialist in the office is and introduce you to him.

SUMMARY

In this book explicit details for an option writing program have been described and illustrated. In addition, the analytical aspects of option buying have been covered. It has been the intent that the reader of this book should know as much about options as is possible to know without actual practice. If the reader has absorbed the contents he will know more about options and the theory that underlies their uses than most brokers. Some of the material in this book is based on research not previously published and the coverage of the opportunities with CBOE options is as up to date as possible. The book has tried to be analytical without being mathematical. This is sometimes difficult and the reader who is interested in the technicalities of supporting research is directed to the references at the end of the book.

When the time is right and the investor is sure, few investment tools can be as profitable as the purchase of options. Whatever the investment climate, the individual willing to ignore the temporary opportunities of speculative ventures and settle for a continual above average return on investment should be enthusiastic about the opportunities of programmed writing. In either case this book has provided a strong background. All that remains is the confidence that comes from some experience. Start slowly, but start soon.

REFERENCES

1. Quantitative Decision Systems, Inc. provides two weekly services, one for option writers and one for option buyers. The services analyze the variability of stocks and provide a rating for options based on premium compared to variability (risk). For information write to: *Quantitative Decision Systems, Inc. P.O. Box 2936, Chicago, Ill. 60690.*

2. Fisher Black and Myron Scholes, "The Valuation of Option Contracts and a Test of Market Efficiency," *Journal of Finance*, 27 (May 1972): 399-417.

3. James A. Boness, "Some Evidence of the Profitability of Trading in Put and Call Options," in Paul H. Cootner, ed., *The Random Character of Stock Market Prices*, Cambridge, Mass: MIT Press, 1964, 475-496.

4. Jerome Bracken, "Models for Call Option Decisions," *Financial Analysts Journal*, 24 (Sept. 1968): 149-151.

5. James B. Cloonan, "A Simulation Study of Strategies for Writing Stock Options," *Proceedings of the Southeastern Regional Meeting of The Institute of Management Sciences 1973.*

6. Richard Katz, "The Profitability of Put and Call Writing," *Industrial Management Review*, 5 (Fall 1963): 55-69.

7. Richard J. Kruizenga, "An Introduction to the Option Contract," in Paul H. Cootner, ed., *The Random Character of Stock Market Prices*, Cambridge, Mass.: MIT Press, 1964, 377-391.

8. Richard J. Kruizenga, "Profit Returns from Purchasing Puts and Calls," in Paul H. Cootner, ed., *The Random Character of Stock Market Prices*, Cambridge, Mass.: MIT Press, 1964, 392-411.

9. Burton G. Malkiel and Richard E. Quandt. *Strategies and Rational Decisions in the Securities Option Market.* Cambridge, Mass.: MIT Press, 1969.

10. Howard M. Taylor, "Evaluating A Call Option and Optimal Timing Strategy in the Stock Market," *Management Science*, 14 (Sept. 1967): 111-120.

GLOSSARY

Away From Market — When the striking price of an option is different than the market price.

Call — A contract giving the buyer the right to buy stock from the writer at a specific price for a set period of time.

CBOE — The Chicago Board Options Exchange.

Certainty — The circumstance when an activity is known to have a specific result.

Conversion (Converting Puts) — The approach used to change a put into a call. The converter accomplishes this by buying a put, selling a call, and buying the underlying stock.

Expected (Profit, Loss) — A term used for probabilistic outcomes. It indicates the average expectation over a large number of trials.

In the Money — An "away from the market" option is "in the money" if the market price of the stock is higher than the striking price for a call and lower than the striking price for a put.

Model — An artificial representation of a real life process. Most interest, relative to investments, is in mathematical models.

NYSE — The New York Stock Exchange.

OTC — Over-the-counter. Refers to options not listed on an exchange.

Probabilistic — The circumstance when an activity is known to result in any one of a number of outcomes and the chance of each outcome is known.

Stock Options

Probability Distribution (pD) — The display of all possible outcomes from a probabilistic event with their probabilities of occurring.

Put — A contract giving the buyer the right to sell stock to the writer at a specific price for a set period of time.

Straddle — A put and a call on the same stock with the same terms.

Strap — Two calls and a put on the same stock with the same terms.

Strip — Two puts and a call on the same stock with the same terms.

Uncertainty — The circumstances when the possible results of an activity are unknown or when the probabilities of the results are unknown.

Writer — The seller of a stock option.